Rua Aquilino Ribeiro L280,

Pontinha, Lisbon

1675-292 PT

+351-968621883

www.UI5CN.com

1. The main category of the book — COMPUTERS > Enterprise Applications > General

TECHNOLOGY & ENGINEERING.

2. Another subject category — COMPUTERS > Web > Web Services & APIs

First Edition

Learn Simple

# Free Gift Coupons

**Or**
**Go here**

# You Might Be Also Interested In

Learn D3.js Simple Way

Internet of Things with SAP HANA:
Build Your IoT Use Case With
Raspberry PI, Arduino Uno, HANA
XSJS and SAPUI5

Learn SAP® UI5: The new enterprise
Javascript framework with examples

SAP® Netweaver Gateway: Learn
how to use SAP® Netweaver
Gateway for UI5 and ABAP projects

# Contents

# 1. Introduction

## 1.1. Data visualization

Data visualization is very popular in recent market place. Google Trends and Analytics are the best examples for Data visualization and its popularity. Data increases cumulatively day by day, and it is difficult to analyse data without effective visualization. Even top businesses do not step into decisions without analysing the data. This is why effective data visualization is a much demanded skill.

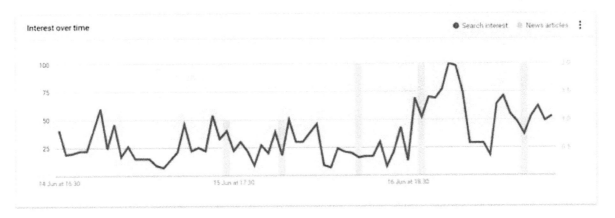

In this book we are going to see the process of visualization and a simple case study. Using the case study we build our own visualization. Also, we will use UX principles to improve our output. At the end of the course you will have a clear understanding about the process and steps that you need to create a perfect visual. One important thing to create a wonderful and nice looking result is the user experience part. It is more like an art than science. The final output of the design in creating the visualization is the combination of Art and Science. The user experience to make the result simple and beautiful is an Art. The process of gathering data, information and using it in your visualization is the science part.

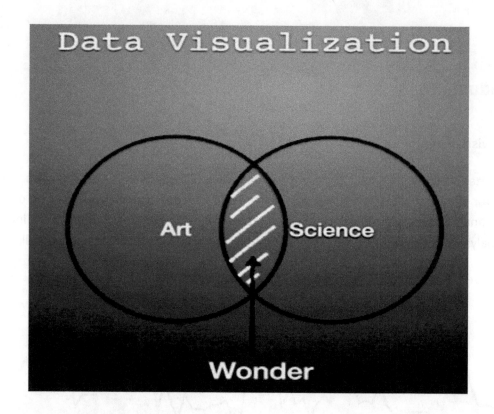

Before going to start the process of data visualization we should always have three things clearly defined. Those three things are:

- **Audience**

- **Scope**

- **Result**

**Audience:** Creating the visualization for specific targeted groups of people.

**Scope:** The scope is the objective that we are actually going to do in our project.

**Result:** The outcome of the project.

These three critical factors form the core purpose of the visualization procedure.

## 1.2. Purpose Statement

In this chapter we will see the purpose statement and check out the differences between good and worse purpose statements.

**Worst Purpose Statements:** The objective is to create a visualization to allow users to answer any question about sales and marketing in visual format. Here it is telling only the outcome of the statement, i.e sales and marketing. It only tells about the outcome that the user will answer the questions about sales and marketing. It is not clear at all on who will be our user and also the scope about the project. The data involved provides no description about considerations while creating sales and marketing visuals.

**Bad Purpose Statements:** By adding a scope to the worst purpose statement we improve it to a bad purpose statement. In this purpose statement, we build a dashboard that will have sales and marketing info of customers, product line, region and store. Here we added a scope. We are clearly saying that considering customers, product line, region and store information in this dashboard. Still we are having one missing point that who will be consuming this dashboard.

**Good Purpose Statement:** The final purpose statement is to provide tools to sales and marketing executives in order to help them make a buying decision, by visualizing the top 5 KPI's, for the past three years, of customers, product line, region and store. In this purpose statement we have all the three necessary components. Here we can clearly recognize who is your target user that is sales and marketing executives. Outcome is the buying decision. The scope here is the past 3 years of customers, product line, region and store.

One more thing that makes the purpose statement even more important is when you are involving in the visualization process then you have to take lot of decisions. It may be big or small decisions. At that time the purpose statement will keep you to track because it is very easy to lose sight of doing the process for what and why? For example, you need to decide about what is the data that should be considered while building the visualization. Should it be real time, near real time or the latency should be involved. Taking decisions about technology should be like whether your technology would be consumed in mobiles, tablet or only on desktop environment? Also, you need to assign what are the tools that user will go to use. For example, the data is to be consumed over excel sheets or Web. Some of the readymade tools like Tableau or Qlikview or you have to use the libraries to write programs for your visualization.

So these decisions are very easy to take if you have set a clear purpose and vision for the project. Generally people will ask questions like, by having such rigid boundaries around my visualization project will it hamper the creativity and innovation side of design and development of the project ? The answer is the main goal here should be to meet the meet the purpose for the visualization made. It is crucial that we must set the purpose statement before starting the visualization project.

You can also check our Learn Data Visualization and Become Data Analyst video course for accelerated learning here or use the below QR code for 50-90% off.

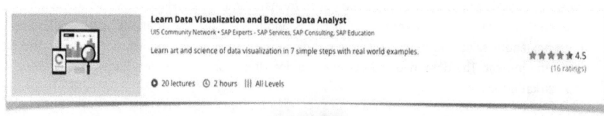

**Learn Data Visualization and Become Data Analyst**
UIS Community Network • SAP Experts - SAP Services, SAP Consulting, SAP Education

Learn art and science of data visualization in 7 simple steps with real world examples.

★★★★★ 4.5
(16 ratings)

● 20 lectures   ⏱ 2 hours   ⫴ All Levels

## 2. Seven Steps of Visualization

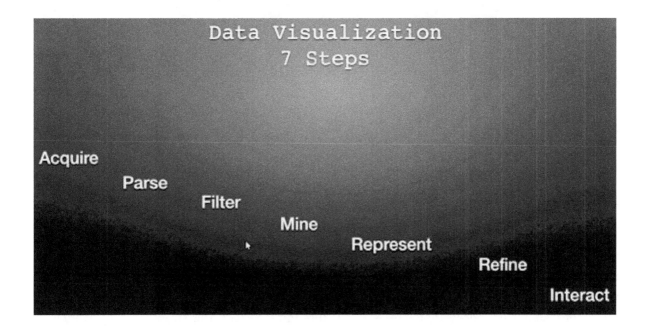

The seven steps of data visualization are:

- Acquire

- Parse

- Filter

- Mine

- Represent

- Refine

- Interact

### 2.1. Acquire

We obtain the data from multiple sources. It can be online or offline files. It may be in multiple formats like text, string or images. Once we acquired the necessary data for our project the next step is parsing.

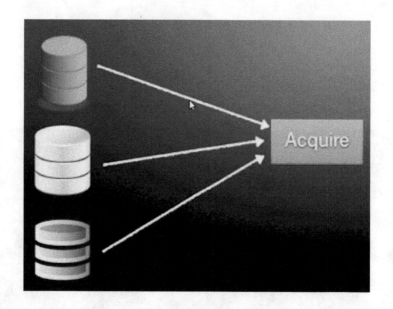

## 2.2. Parse

In this stage we are going to provide some structure to the data. The data acquired in the parse may or may not have any structure. In this stage we need to provide it. We are not going to build relational record here. So it is not necessary to create a structure to be perfect. This structure or category is only provided to the data so that we can operate on them with consecutive steps.

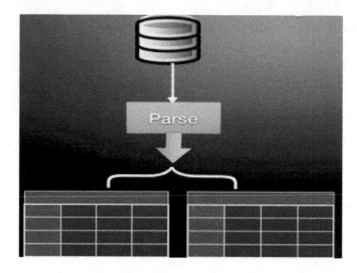

## 2.3. Filter
In filter stage we will remove all the unwanted data and keep the data that is relevant for our project.

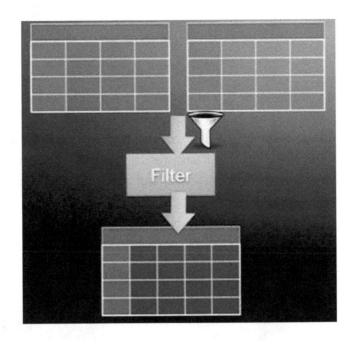

## 2.4. Mine

Here you may have to implement statistics and data mining concepts here. The main goal is to find any **patterns**. Once you are able to identify the patterns among data points. It is very easy to explain when they are mapped in charts or graphs.

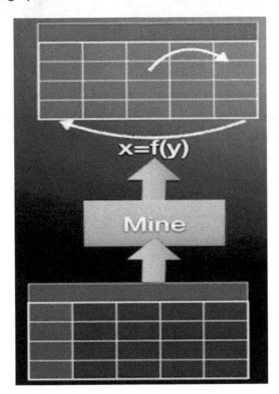

## 2.5. Represent

Using the data points we will represent it into graphs or charts. The example given below shows a bubble chart. But, it can be any chart or combination of one or more charts. If you are creating a dashboard then it contains lot of charts or KPI. It can also happen that if we are merging lot of chart types into a single chart. This is also an important transition phase from data scientist to an artistic mindset. After this we need to care about aesthetics and beauty of data visualization. It can also be referred as the User Experience.

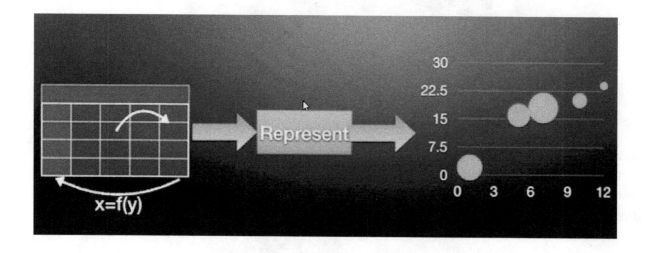

## 2.6. Refine

Once we represented data into charts or maps then we can do start refining those. The last two steps are Refine and Interact. We iterate through lot of variations of how the final design should look like. We constantly improve the final data visualization and also user interaction with data visualization besides its functionality with purpose statement.

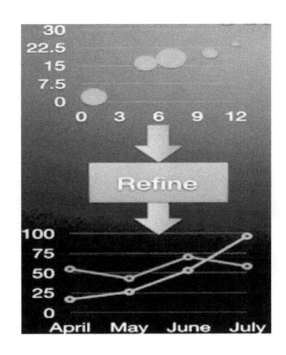

## 2.7. Interact

This step considers about the user interaction with the data visualization.

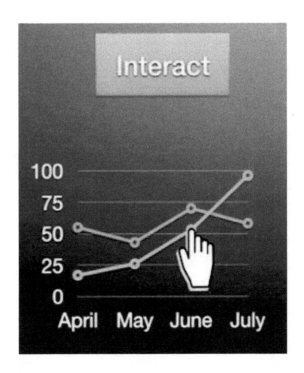

15

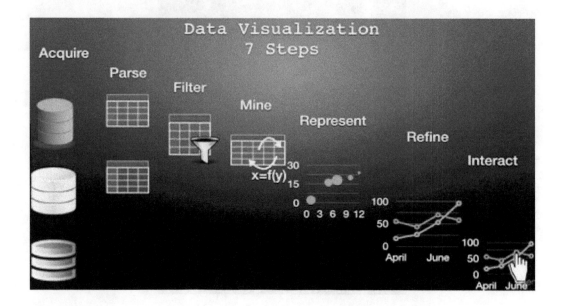

In coming sections we will see the example of data visualization using these 7steps. Then you will get a better understanding about the 7 steps process.

You can also check our Learn Data Visualization and Become Data Analyst video course for accelerated learning here or use the below QR code for 50-90% off.

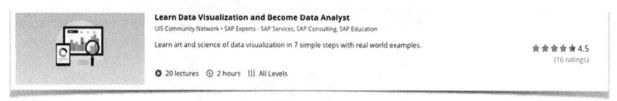

# 3. Types of data Visualization

In the previous section, we saw the 7 steps of data visualization. To reach the final step we need to do a series of intermediate steps and these steps require lot of decisions to be made. The purpose statement will help to take those decisions and stay on right path.

Every visualization is different. But depending upon its purpose statements we can categorize them in three different types. It is important to know the three main groups. This is because once you know the type of visualization you are dealing, then, it will be very easy to take those intermediate decisions. Sometimes, it will be useful to move backwards from the final result that will be ideal delivery for the project. The three different categories of visualization are

- Strategic

- Operational

- Tactical

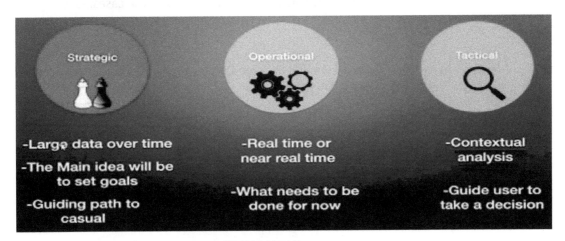

## 3.1. Strategic

The main characteristic of this visualization type is to help users to take strategic decisions. They mostly deal with strategy and more interested in seeing large data over time. The main idea is the users looking for patterns for establishing the goals. We have to guide our user to a casual idea or an action. Here we have to tell the user about the actions we have to place because they will be well aware of the action A corresponds to Action B. If they are interested in suppressing the action they will avoid in future events or if they want to promote it they can promote it as well.

## 3.2. Operational

The operational type can be real time or near real time. For example, imagine there is a warehouse; the warehouse manager wants to know about the flow rate. So, he can perform some action if it is low or below some critical point. The main goal is to understand the situation and take those decisions in current time. Most of the KPI based dashboards which we will see in dashboard comes in operational category.

## 3.3. Tactical

The final category is the tactical type. Here we will do lot of contextual analysis. We are guiding our user to take a decision that may require some analysis. The amount of analysis comes under the range of strategic and operation type. In strategic type we have to spend a lot of time in analysing the situation to come up with a good strategy. In operational strategy we may not require any strategy at all. In tactical we are in between those two categories. One of the popular examples for tactical type is root cause analysis. The users will find the root cause problem by analysing the events processes and people.

During working on a visualization project it may consist of one or more of these cases.

You can also check our Learn Data Visualization and Become Data Analyst video course for accelerated learning here or use the below QR code for 50-90% off.

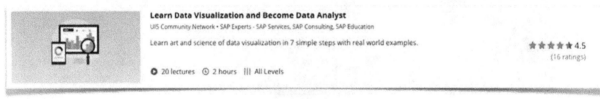

**Learn Data Visualization and Become Data Analyst**
UI5 Community Network • SAP Experts - SAP Services, SAP Consulting, SAP Education

Learn art and science of data visualization in 7 simple steps with real world examples.

★ ★ ★ ★ ★ 4.5
(16 ratings)

● 20 lectures  ⊙ 2 hours  ||| All Levels

# 4. Creating Wireframe for final output

In previous section we saw how we can have a requirement or purpose statement that can involve more than one category. Let's look into a simple example. In this example, we have a wireframe of the final design. Here we can see the visualization consists of three KPIs, one table with detailed information, a pie chart and a time graph. Using the slider under the time graph we can zoom out to see on a year basis. Also, you can see the trend over time and zoom in to see in hourly basis too. The slider can provide a wide range to our X-Axis (Time scale) and the timeline is used to meet strategic needs.

If we are using the trends over time and want to develop a plan over a new strategy for the action then we will use the time graph.

We may be taking some operational decisions. For example in the KPI tiles, the value reaches below certain level then the user can take immediate actions. Those actions come under operational requirements. Most of the time the data fades for operational requirements will be real time or near real time.

It also illustrates when we are working in a tactical analysis and not going into detail. We need just feedback or information to tackle a problem. The very common example we give is the root cause analysis over the issues our business might be having. Altogether this is our visualization that involves one or more different categories of visualizations. Most of the times while getting these type of requirements involving multiple categories of visualization we easily tend to get overwhelmed. At this point of time we need to follow divide and conquer approach. We have to divide each individual purpose statements separately. Once we have a separate purpose statement clearly then it becomes very easy to follow the 7 steps of data visualization.

What happens if we have two or more categories present in our visualization project? It is very common that we will have a core present in the project. It can be a single feature having more impact than all the other features combined. This is not a new thing, the same over the 80/20 rule also known as a Plato Principle. We need to focus little more on the core and give more time compared to other features.

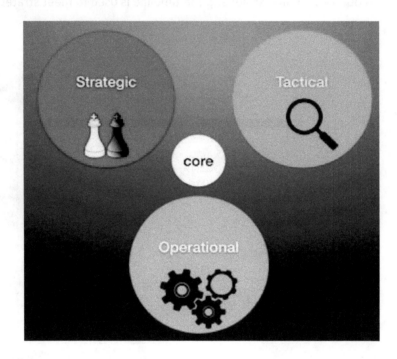

To identify the core we have to ask the right questions. What is the feature present in my visualization that has maximum impact in user decision making process? Which feature will influence the key take away from my visualization to the user?

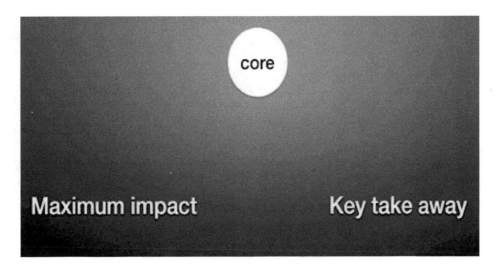

One very important point before going into the details of 7 stages of visualization is "It is all about data". Any fancy or cool looking visualization graphs or charts would not steal the show if it does not tally with the purpose statement. That is a common mistake people do. We should be focused on representing the data instead of depending on the graphical design capabilities.

In this section let's explore the process by looking into a simple example. Initially we are going to take a purpose statement. In this purpose statement we need to understand the three main important parts Audience, Scope and Outcome that it has. If we read the purpose statement it says that we need to "Build a dashboard which will be utilized by people monitoring population growth of different states of US, so they can allocate resource to states based upon current population and population growth of these states."

**Who is the audience that we are creating visualization for?**

People who needs to monitor population growth. Now, we are clear about that.

**How the visualization is going to help our audience?**

If we see that, the people who are monitoring population growth have to allocate resources to the individual state. So this data visualization project must help them to allocate resources for individual state according to the population.

**What is the scope of the project?**

We have kept the use case fairly simple by only involving the current population and population growth of the state. With those data our users will be taking the decisions to allocate new resources to the states. Combining altogether we will get the final outcome of the project. Now we have the purpose statement ready.

## Purpose/Requirements

**Audience**

"Build a dashboard which will be utilised by people who monitors population growth of different states of US,so they can allocate resources to states based upon current population and population growth of these state."

**Outcome**

**Scope**

You can also check our Learn Data Visualization and Become Data Analyst video course for accelerated learning here or use the below QR code for 50-90% off.

**Learn Data Visualization and Become Data Analyst**
UIS Community Network • SAP Experts - SAP Services, SAP Consulting, SAP Education

Learn art and science of data visualization in 7 simple steps with real world examples.

★★★★★ 4.5
(16 ratings)

▶ 20 lectures    ⏱ 2 hours    ⫴ All Levels

# 5. Mapping the Steps

Using this purpose statement we are going to create a simple visualization project. The first step is the **Acquire** phase.

## 5.1. Acquire data

In Acquire phase we are going to collect data from different sources. To give you an example: We can go into customer database. In this case we have to go to census database and collect the data for population. It can be an excel format, CSV, JSON or XML. Here we are going to show you the process by downloading the file offline and then processing the record. However, in real time the application will get data that will query from the server or database. Here we are not going to do any hard coded data.

One thing we have to understand. Once we have created the visualization for the requirement, the integration to database queries can be done later on as well. Only thing that we need to make sure is that the data we are going to work on can be granted from the sources. Example, If we are designing an operational dashboard then in the acquire phase we get the data from a database that we are not able to query directly. In the project many times the operational dashboard need to be in real time or near real time. In these cases it is better to avoid those data sources where we cannot have integration with the front end and back end. In this case study we are not going to do integration in detail. It contains more technical terms and depends upon the technology we are working on.

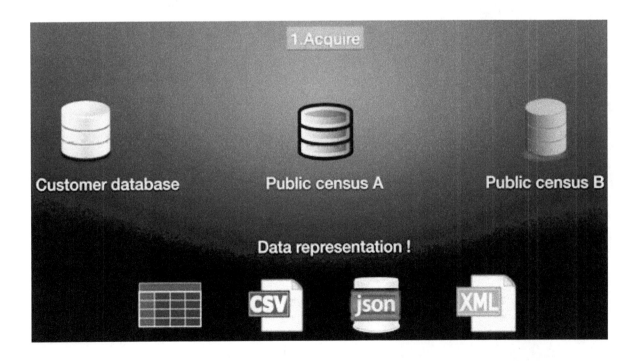

So we need to acquire data that is needed for our project. For that we will collect it from the sources and save those in an offline file for our project. For this project we are going to collect data about the US population. So we can go to US Census Bureau website and collect the data.

**Steps to acquire data**

1. Go to US Census website http://www.census.gov/ . In the homepage we can see that 2015 Population Estimate and components of population change. Click on it.

2.

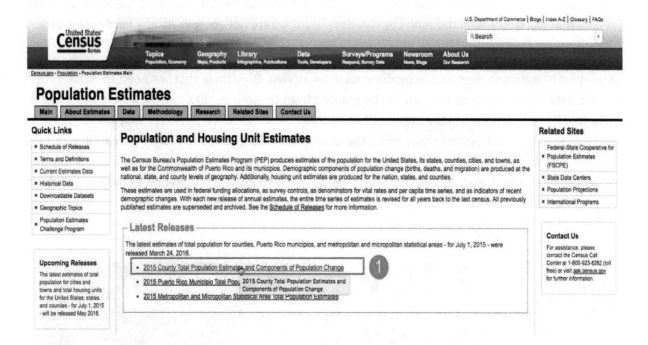

3. In the next page we have to go to Annual Population Estimates.

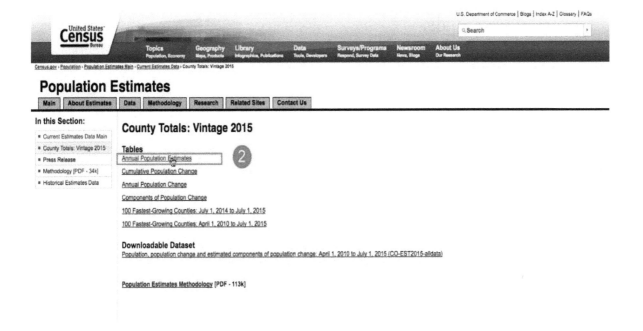

4. After that in the next page we can see that state names. It contains the data by state wise. We need data for all states. So at the bottom of the page we will select 'All States' to collect data.

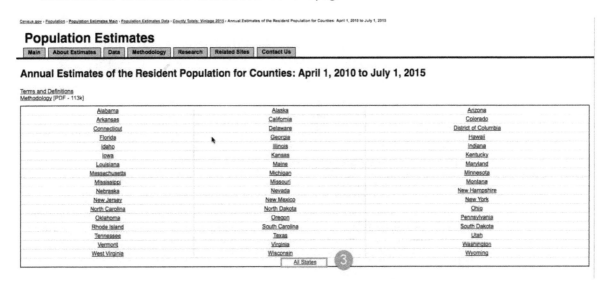

5. It will go to next page and display the data. We have an option to download the data. Click on it then it will ask for options.

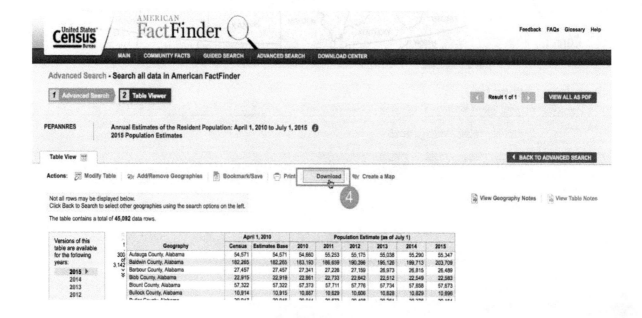

6. We need excel data so click on 'Microsoft Excel (.xls)' format and click ok. It will take some time to display the download option. Then click on the download option that appears after certain time.

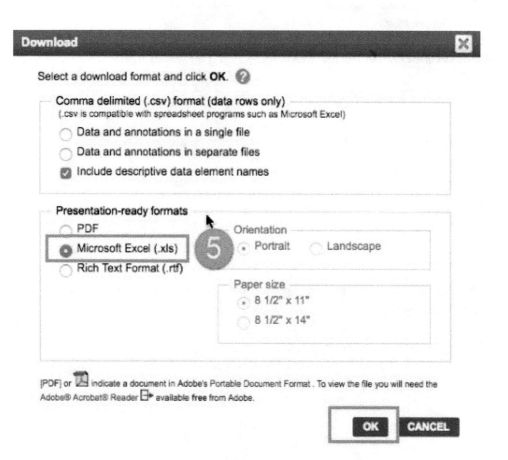

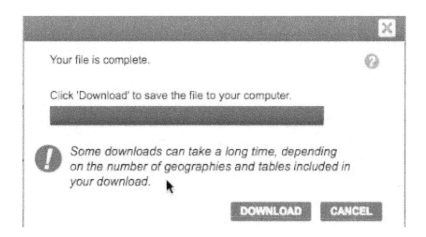

7.  After we get the file open it and export it into CSV file. CSV is comma separated file that will be used in most of applications.

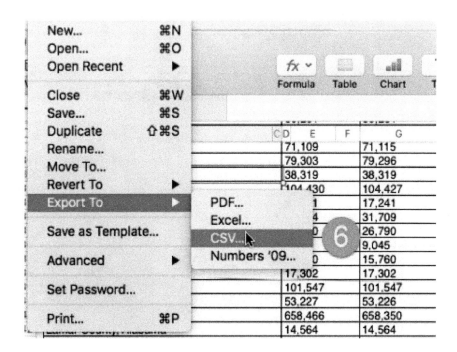

Here in this file we have multiple entries of each county. We have to aggregate the counties to get the data for state. There are subsequent steps in the visualization process for performing those actions. In this table we have the population estimate for the year 2011, 2012, 2013, 2014, and 2015. We may require data for the current year. However, in census website we are not able to get the current year data. So we need a mathematical model to predict the current population. It will be done in the later phases.

The CSV file will look like this when you open it in any text editor.

```
data of us population.csv

pie demo1.js  ×   bubbleChart.html  ×   pie chart.html  ×   lineChart.html  ×   lineChartCompatible.html  ×

25    ,Minnesota,325563,269743,595306,1190612,
26    ,Mississippi,261050,235919,496969,993938,
27    ,Missouri,197962,148467,346429,692858,
28    ,Montana,292296,360164,652460,1304920,
29    ,Nebraska,169713,148298,318011,636022,
30    ,Nevada,366190,340282,706472,1412944,
31    ,New Hampshire,186506,344325,530831,1061662,
32    ,New Jersey,320955,187453,508408,1016816,
33    ,New Mexico,199857,199857,399714,799428,
34    ,New York,364050,364050,728100,1456200,
35    ,North Carolina,343249,343249,686498,1372996,
36    ,North Dakota,178921,178921,357842,715684,
37    ,Ohio,387823,387823,775646,1551292,
38    ,Oklahoma,257672,257672,515344,1030688,
39    ,Oregon,233726,233726,467452,934904,
40    ,Pennsylvania,51114,51114,102228,204456,
41    ,Rhode Island,175125,175125,350250,700500,
42    ,South Carolina,219089,219089,438178,876356,
43    ,South Dakota,208980,208980,417960,835920,
44    ,Tennessee,93812,93812,187624,375248,
45    ,Texas,335840,335840,671680,1343360,
46    ,Utah,78393,78393,156786,313572,
47    ,Vermont,336011,336011,672022,1344044,
48    ,Virginia,365321,365321,730642,1461284,
49    ,Washington,300150,300150,600300,1200600,
50    ,West Virginia,109914,109914,219828,439656,
51    ,Wisconsin,200250,200250,400500,801000,
52    ,Wyoming,338413,338413,676826,1353652,
53    ,Puerto Rico,154843,154843,309686,619372,
```

Before moving to the next phase we will see a nice tool called 'Mr. Data Converter'.

URL: http://shancarter.github.io/mr-data-converter/

This is the very useful tool to convert data on the fly. It can convert data into different web friendly formats. For example, we have the excel file. Import this file into a CSV file by selecting the option import in excel sheet. Now, we got a CSV file which is a comma separated file from the excel table. Open the CSV file using any text editor. Simply copy the contents and paste it into the Mr. Data Converter and select the format that you want to convert. Here we are going to convert it into JSON Property format. Select the JSON property and hit enter. Now you can get the JSON data without need of any additional software.

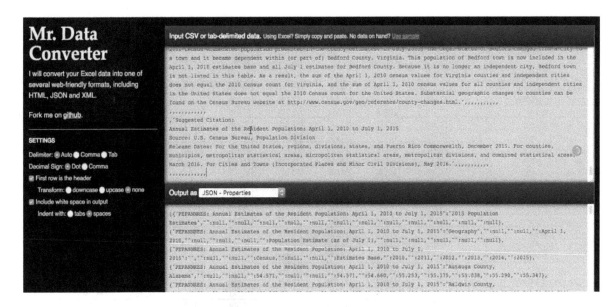

In the next step we are going to work with data that we acquired. The next phase is the filtering process where we are going to remove unnecessary data. In some cases we may require additional data. In those situations we need to come back to acquire phase and collect the data. One of the very popular examples is using a map. We collected all the information of the states but in design stage we may need to add co-ordinates and sequencing to the map. So those data points need to be acquired then we have to return to Acquire state to collect data.

## 5.2. Parse data

Now we have managed to get some data to start with our project. Sometimes, we are working on a project with huge files and they can be different types of data files that we require. It may not be only Excel or CSV file. It can be XML JSON or text file. Therefore, we have to categorise those data files into some structure and we can start working on that. This second step is called the parsing phase as you already know.

| PEPANNRES: Annual Estimates of the 2015 Population Estimates | | | | | | | | |
|---|---|---|---|---|---|---|---|---|
| Geography | April 1, 2010 | | Population Estimate (as of July 1) | | | | | |
| | Census | Estimates | 2010 | 2011 | 2012 | 2013 | 2014 | 2015 |
| Autauga County, Alabama | 54,571 | 54,571 | 54,660 | 55,253 | 55,175 | 55,038 | 55,290 | 55,347 |
| Baldwin County, Alabama | 182,265 | 182,265 | 183,193 | 186,659 | 190,396 | 195,126 | 199,713 | 203,709 |
| Barbour County, Alabama | 27,457 | 27,457 | 27,341 | 27,226 | 27,159 | 26,973 | 26,815 | 26,489 |
| Bibb County, Alabama | 22,915 | 22,919 | 22,861 | 22,733 | 22,642 | 22,512 | 22,549 | 22,583 |
| Blount County, Alabama | 57,322 | 57,322 | 57,373 | 57,711 | 57,776 | 57,734 | 57,658 | 57,673 |
| Bullock County, Alabama | 10,914 | 10,915 | 10,887 | 10,629 | 10,606 | 10,628 | 10,829 | 10,696 |
| Butler County, Alabama | 20,947 | 20,946 | 20,944 | 20,673 | 20,408 | 20,261 | 20,276 | 20,154 |
| Calhoun County, Alabama | 118,572 | 118,586 | 118,437 | 117,768 | 117,286 | 116,575 | 115,993 | 115,620 |
| Chambers County, Alabama | 34,215 | 34,170 | 34,098 | 33,993 | 34,075 | 34,153 | 34,052 | 34,123 |
| Cherokee County, Alabama | 25,989 | 25,986 | 25,976 | 26,080 | 26,023 | 26,084 | 25,995 | 25,859 |
| Chilton County, Alabama | 43,643 | 43,631 | 43,665 | 43,739 | 43,697 | 43,795 | 43,921 | 43,943 |
| Choctaw County, Alabama | 13,859 | 13,858 | 13,841 | 13,593 | 13,543 | 13,378 | 13,289 | 13,170 |
| Clarke County, Alabama | 25,833 | 25,840 | 25,767 | 25,570 | 25,144 | 25,116 | 24,847 | 24,675 |
| Clay County, Alabama | 13,932 | 13,932 | 13,880 | 13,670 | 13,456 | 13,467 | 13,538 | 13,555 |
| Cleburne County, Alabama | 14,972 | 14,972 | 14,973 | 14,971 | 14,921 | 15,028 | 15,072 | 15,018 |
| Coffee County, Alabama | 49,948 | 49,948 | 50,177 | 50,448 | 51,173 | 50,755 | 50,831 | 51,211 |
| Colbert County, Alabama | 54,428 | 54,428 | 54,514 | 54,443 | 54,472 | 54,471 | 54,480 | 54,354 |
| Conecuh County, Alabama | 13,228 | 13,228 | 13,208 | 13,121 | 12,996 | 12,875 | 12,662 | 12,672 |
| Coosa County, Alabama | 11,539 | 11,758 | 11,758 | 11,348 | 11,195 | 11,059 | 10,807 | 10,724 |
| Covington County, Alabama | 37,765 | 37,765 | 37,796 | 38,060 | 37,818 | 37,830 | 37,888 | 37,835 |
| Crenshaw County, Alabama | 13,906 | 13,906 | 13,853 | 13,896 | 13,951 | 13,932 | 13,948 | 13,963 |
| Cullman County, Alabama | 80,406 | 80,410 | 80,473 | 80,469 | 80,374 | 80,756 | 81,221 | 82,005 |
| Dale County, Alabama | 50,251 | 50,251 | 50,358 | 50,109 | 50,324 | 49,833 | 49,501 | 49,565 |

This is the data file we acquired from the acquire phase. We want to assign the data into different types in parsing phase. The categorization happens in parse phase. In the next phase we will be removing the non essential parts of the data. One question may arise is why we are not aggregating the data. Here we require data required for state and not for county. The general answer is, either we can perform this step in the parsing phase or we can wait until the mining phase. There we will be finding the relationship between the data points and will also be doing aggregation and separation accordingly. The next phase is the filtering phase to remove unwanted data.

## 5.3. How to filter data ?

In the filtering step we are going to reduce the data by removing the data points that are not required in our visualization. What would we do if we removed one data point and later on we need that? It is very common happening in data visualization. In filtering stage people are doubtful on removing data because we cannot be sure that the data might or might not be needed on later point. Note here, we are making decision in the process depending upon which type of project we are working. We might be working in a project where we have specific instructions or as per purpose statement to deliver it to customers.

Also, in this scenario it is very common that we will be having access to business analyst or functional consultant. These are the people having domain knowledge. Example, if we are using this use case that we are currently working, then the functional consultant or analyst might have some experience dealing with census data before. In these positions people having both domain experience and technical experience are preferred instead of only having technical experience. This is because, it will be much easier to work with them and the users or customers don't have to do much of hand holding to someone with experience working on the field. Now, the other scenario can be that we have complete freedom to explore and innovate but the solution should meet its purpose. In the current use case let us assume that we are in the middle ground here. We have both domain experience and also given freedom to think relatively in the project.

This is the simple sketch that we are going to perform. It is a two dimensional table data we might finally require. The columns are years (Even number of years denoted here). We put this because sometimes we need to put boundaries to filter our data.

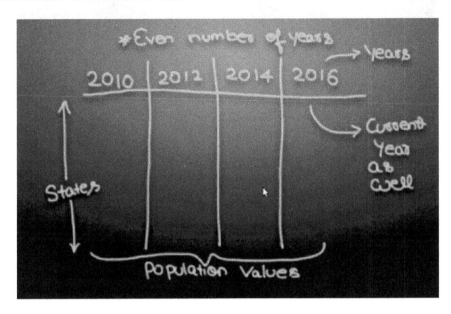

For example, in the census example, the decisions to allocate resources to states are made on alternative years (not every year). So, we need to consider an even number of years. This is one type of condition that we face on our projects. This condition is just an example to demonstrate that. We need to filter the data based on certain requirements like these. The filtering condition in our case is for even number of years. In the rows we can see data on individual states and we have also introduced the current year. As per our purpose statement the decision will depend upon the population growth and population of current year.

In the table data we collected from the census website contains numbers until 2015 only. So we need to predict the data using some mathematical calculations and also we need to do aggregation to combine all counties that are in the same state. This we are going to do in mining phase which is the next phase after filter phase.

## 5.4. How to mine data for Patterns?

Mining is the next official step after filtering the data. The goal is to find relationship among data points which are required in the visualization. This relationship can be a mathematical representation based on the requirement. In our case the example was to predict the current year. The input will be the population of the previous number of years.

31

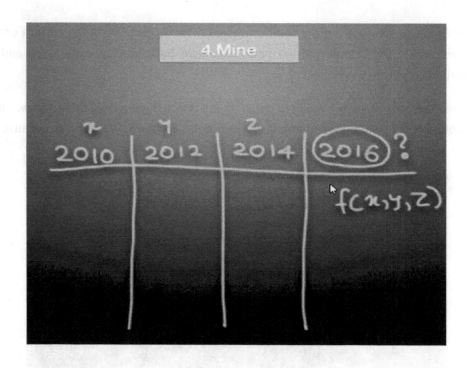

We need to know one thing before actually doing the operations. The next step after mining is representing. Sometimes mining is dependent upon what we are representing. We must have to derive new data like the population for current year. Another example is where you decide to plot our state vs. population graph.

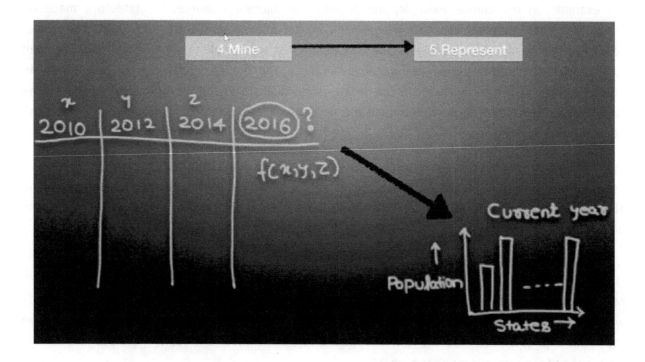

32

If we decide to change the graph instead of population we need population density. Then we need to calculate population density using formula.

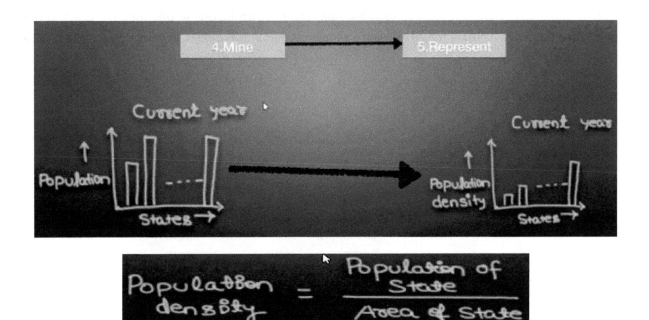

To do this we need to go to the first phase that is the acquire phase to gather the area of the state. Then come back to this mine stage to do these operations. Then we need to draw bar charts. Here we are going to more backward stages. It is a very frequent circumstance in visualization project.

Next we need to filter the data. Actually it has to be done in filter stage but we need to aggregate some data so we are doing it after the mining stage. Simply go to the table and delete the data that are not needed for us.

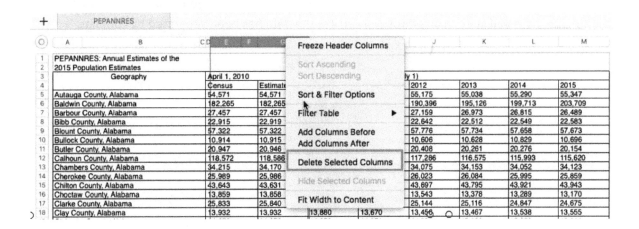

33

After removing the unwanted data we need to aggregate the data of all states. First we have to separate the county name and state name. Then we need to add all the records which have the same state. After seeing the final result of aggregation this is the final table shown below. In this we have years in the column. We also have the data for 2016 using a simple mathematical model. In rows we have state with its corresponding data.

| Name | 2010 | 2012 | 2014 | 2016 |
|---|---|---|---|---|
| Alabama | 171889 | 305360 | 477249 | 954498 |
| Alaska | 366915 | 192876 | 559791 | 1119582 |
| Arizona | 161698 | 167019 | 328717 | 657434 |
| Arkansas | 225047 | 167890 | 392937 | 785874 |
| California | 181019 | 375244 | 556263 | 1112526 |
| Colorado | 343408 | 325563 | 668971 | 1337942 |
| Connecticut | 207191 | 261050 | 468241 | 936482 |
| Delaware | 214378 | 197962 | 412340 | 824680 |
| District of Columbia | 154294 | 292296 | 446590 | 893180 |
| Florida | 370712 | 169713 | 540425 | 1080850 |
| Georgia | 269743 | 366190 | 635933 | 1271866 |
| Hawaii | 235919 | 186506 | 422425 | 844850 |
| Idaho | 148467 | 320955 | 469422 | 938844 |
| Illinois | 360164 | 171889 | 532053 | 1064106 |
| Indiana | 148298 | 366915 | 515213 | 1030426 |
| Iowa | 340282 | 161698 | 501980 | 1003960 |

**Note:** The data is generated mostly using the steps we have seen. But some data points are randomly selected where you are not able to see the exact data points we collected from census website. This is because of the legal stand point of this course. We don't want users to come into conclusion in representation phase. So we are playing with randomly generated data, but you have to assume that it is the real data using in our project.

Next step is to export the data by go to file> export to> CSV. Once you exported it into a Comma separated file then you open in an editor you can see the data has been separated by commas.

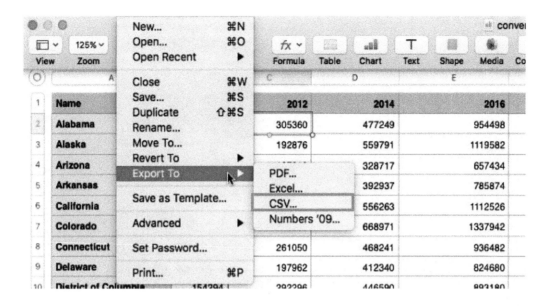

Sometime we also need JSON data files. We convert it into JSON data file using Mr. Data Converter. To do this copy all the contents inside the CSV file and paste it into Mr. Data converter. Then, select the output as JSON to convert it into JSON data. Here it will show some error because of the extra delimiter present in each line (i. e a Comma/,). We need to remove all those to get the exact JSON data. If the volume of the data is very high, we may need to create a JavaScript program to filter these operations or by any third party software available.

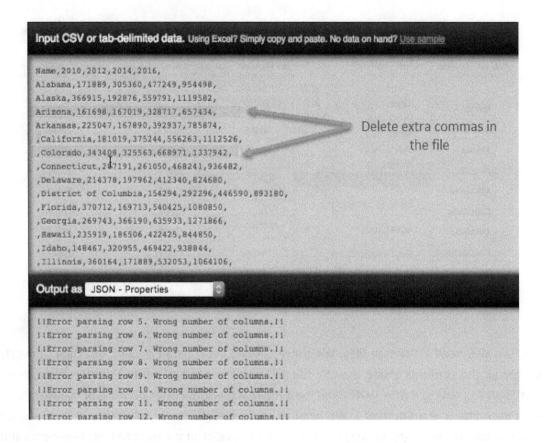

Input CSV or tab-delimited data. Using Excel? Simply copy and paste. No data on hand? Use sample

Name,2010,2012,2014,2016,
Alabama,171889,305360,477249,954498,
Alaska,366915,192876,559791,1119582,
Arizona,161698,167019,328717,657434,
Arkansas,225047,167890,392937,785874,
,California,181019,375244,556263,1112526,
,Colorado,343408,325563,668971,1337942,
,Connecticut,207191,261050,468241,936482,
,Delaware,214378,197962,412340,824680,
,District of Columbia,154294,292296,446590,893180,
,Florida,370712,169713,540425,1080850,
,Georgia,269743,366190,635933,1271866,
,Hawaii,235919,186506,422425,844850,
,Idaho,148467,320955,469422,938844,
,Illinois,360164,171889,532053,1064106,

Delete extra commas in the file

Output as JSON - Properties

!!Error parsing row 5. Wrong number of columns.!!
!!Error parsing row 6. Wrong number of columns.!!
!!Error parsing row 7. Wrong number of columns.!!
!!Error parsing row 8. Wrong number of columns.!!
!!Error parsing row 9. Wrong number of columns.!!
!!Error parsing row 10. Wrong number of columns.!!
!!Error parsing row 11. Wrong number of columns.!!
!!Error parsing row 12. Wrong number of columns.!!

After removing the extra delimiters we have the JSON file like this below.

Input CSV or tab-delimited data. Using Excel? Simply copy and paste. No data on hand? Use sample

Nebraska,169713,148298,318011,636022,
Nevada,366190,340282,706472,1412944,
New Hampshire,186506,344325,530831,1061662,
New Jersey,320955,187453,508408,1016816,
New Mexico,199857,199857,399714,799428,
New York,364050,364050,728100,1456200,
North Carolina,343249,343249,686498,1372996,
North Dakota,178921,178921,357842,715684,
Ohio,387823,387823,775646,1551292,
Oklahoma,257672,257672,515344,1030688,
Oregon,233726,233726,467452,934904,
Pennsylvania,51114,51114,102228,204456,
Rhode Island,175125,175125,350250,700500,
South Carolina,219089,219089,438178,876356,
South Dakota,209980,208980,417960,835920,
Tennessee,93812,93812,187624,375248

Output as JSON - Properties

{"Name":"District of Columbia","2010":154294,"2012":292296,"2014":446590,"2016":893180,"":null},
{"Name":"Florida","2010":370712,"2012":169713,"2014":540425,"2016":1080850,"":null},
{"Name":"Georgia","2010":269743,"2012":366190,"2014":635933,"2016":1271866,"":null},
{"Name":"Hawaii","2010":235919,"2012":186506,"2014":422425,"2016":844850,"":null},
{"Name":"Idaho","2010":148467,"2012":320955,"2014":469422,"2016":938844,"":null},
{"Name":"Illinois","2010":360164,"2012":171889,"2014":532053,"2016":1064106,"":null},
{"Name":"Indiana","2010":148298,"2012":366915,"2014":515213,"2016":1030426,"":null},
{"Name":"Iowa","2010":340282,"2012":161698,"2014":501980,"2016":1003960,"":null},
{"Name":"Kansas","2010":344325,"2012":225047,"2014":569372,"2016":1138744,"":null},
{"Name":"Kentucky","2010":187453,"2012":181019,"2014":368472,"2016":736944,"":null},
{"Name":"Louisiana","2010":305360,"2012":343408,"2014":648768,"2016":1297536,"":null},
{"Name":"Maine","2010":192876,"2012":207191,"2014":400067,"2016":800134,"":null},
{"Name":"Maryland","2010":167019,"2012":214378,"2014":381397,"2016":762794,"":null},

Now we can use the JSON file in our project. We are going to use D3 so the JSON file will be required there. You can use CSV file but JSON is popular now a days. As a developer it is very easy to use JSON data files compared to CSV file.

## 5.5. Represent

Most of the user experience phase is defined from our representation phase. When we are working on a visualization that is going to be consumed over web browsers then we have to work in a grid system.

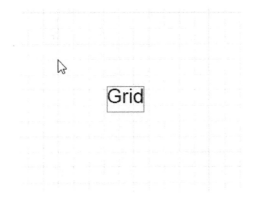

Lot of the wireframing tool uses the grid system so we can identify the components we are going to use. It is a very iterative process and it may take a lot of time.

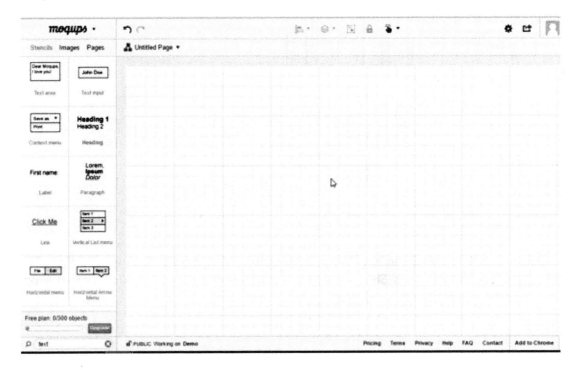

Now we are in the wireframing tool. We are going to use this tool for user interface. Here we need a bar chart. Always try to start with a bar chart as it is the best way to represent. If we have a graph with time factors then we can use the line chart. In the bar chart we need to visualize population over state. In X – Axis we have the state and in Y – Axis we have the population. This bar chart is going to represent population for current year.

To add a bar chart in Moqups, search for 'bar chart' in the search bar provided left hand side below.

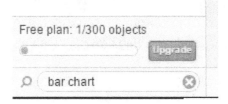

This is the bar chart we created using moqups.

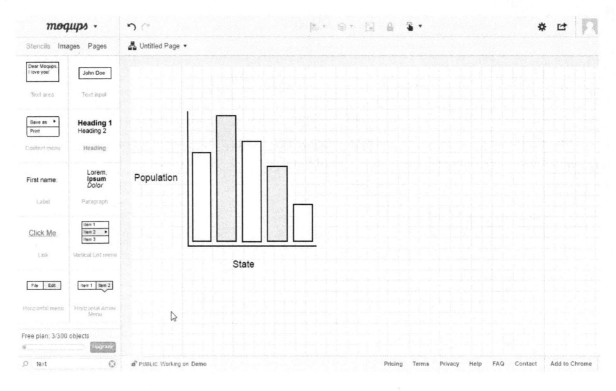

In the right hand side we are going to place map to be interactive enough to represent information to individual states for multiple years. Showing data in a map is very popular and effective that people can see the map of the state with the corresponding information.

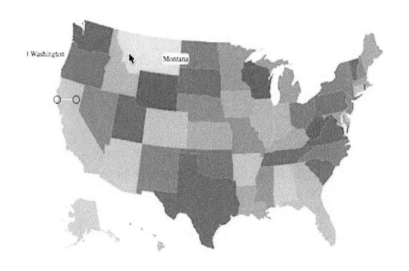

We are also going to add another bar chart. If the user clicks the state then it shows population over year to that specific state. Also a KPI tile is to be added to see the population for current year when the user clicks the state. This is the representation stage where we are deciding the components and elements to select for representing our data. We also need to take decisions like colours and scales to be used and all the little details. The little details actually matter a lot when we see the final user experience of our project.

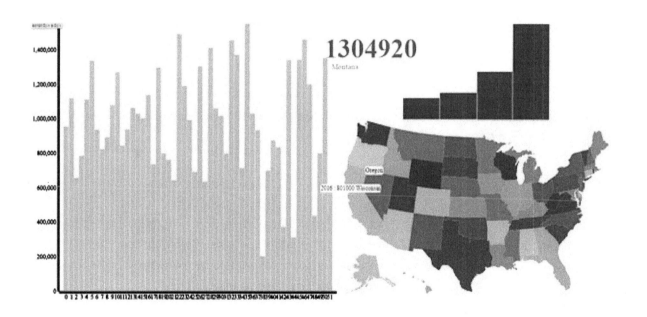

To choose the colour palette we can use the website called http://colorbrewer2.org/

In this website you can use the colour palette used in our project. They can also provide the Hexadecimal code that can be used in our programming language. Also, it provides a final glimpse of what the final palette looks like. It is always better to use the same font for a symmetric and uniform look.

## 5.6. Refine

During refining our visualization we may need to add or remove more charts. While performing this decision we need to know why we are performing that action. Think by purpose statement if we want to add an additional bar chart. Would it be necessary? Are we able to merge with some other charts? For example, we are having two bar charts in our example. Are we able to merge both the bar charts? Consider the fact that it will make the visualization more complex and it is complex to the user also.

These are the steps we are doing in refine stage for delivering better user experience. After our representation phase we need to work on interactions. For example, in the map if we move the mouse over the map then what are the element changes are to happen. If we click on it then what are the changes that are going to happen in the bar charts related to this. Also, if we move the mouse over the bar chart it should show the population over state. These are the planning points that we are going to apply in our project in interaction stage.

Consider the parameter if we are using our mobile phones to represent our visualization. In those cases we need to take care of the responsiveness and also the user events like tap and drag. These details are taken care in the final stage or Interaction stage.

## 5.7. Interact

The two stages refine and interact are interlinked with each other. This is because we are iteratively taking care of adding more charts and more information or else removing the charts that are unnecessary. The main idea is to improve our visualization over time in these stages. Many times we need to go back and forth to achieve perfection in our user interface section.

These are the seven steps of data visualization process and we will see the summary to see what and how we did this.

## 5.8. Summary of 7 Stages

**Acquire**: In this stage we collected data from US Census website

**Parse**: We provided some meaning and structure to the data. In our case we already have a structure of requisite data.

**Filter**: We filtered some data that we did not require. We also added a condition here that we only use even number of years and subsequently filtered out the odd number of years.

**Mine**: According to our purpose statement we required data for current year which is not available in our acquired data. For that we used some mathematical calculation to predict data for current year population depending upon previous years values.

**Represent**: In this stage we picked some basic chart types. We used our wireframing tool for performing these steps.

**Refine and Interact :** In the consecutive steps of refine and interact we improved our visualization. Specifically in interactive stage we also saw how different components in the UI will behave during user interactions. The last three stages are interlinked closely. Refine and interact are iterative process that are generally done parallel.

These are the 7 steps of visualization project. There are lot of back loops will be performed. Example, while we represent the data and if we need to add some additional data. Then we need to go to acquire and filter data.

Also the other common back loop present is where we define interactions. We may need to have more components or refine existing components. So these three stages are in a way an iterative process and consume some time to complete this. One suggestion while working on last three stages (Represent, Refine and Interact) is to spend more time in these stages. This is because the effort will have a lot of impact in our final UI.

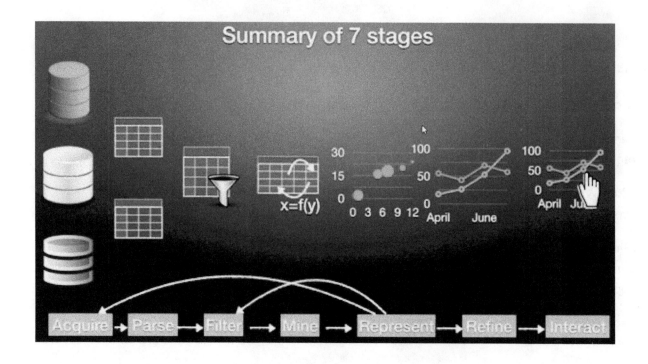

You can also check our Learn Data Visualization and Become Data Analyst video course for accelerated learning here or use the below QR code for 50-90% off.

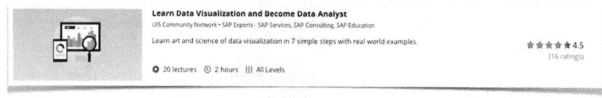

**Learn Data Visualization and Become Data Analyst**
UIS Community Network • SAP Experts - SAP Services, SAP Consulting, SAP Education

Learn art and science of data visualization in 7 simple steps with real world examples.

★ ★ ★ ★ ★ 4.5
(16 ratings)

○ 20 lectures   ⏱ 2 hours   ||| All Levels

# 6. D3 – Data Driven Documents

D3 is an open source JavaScript library. Using D3 we can use wonderful visualization. D3 is very powerful and its possibility is endless. In recent time it has become a de facto standard of visualization.

Let's go into www.d3js.org to know more about this library.

This is the d3js.org homepage. It is an open source library that comes with a BST License. We can use this library for free in our projects. We can go to examples. Here examples are increasing day by day. It contains bubble chart, bar chart bullet charts, etc. There are also lots of innovative charts that people are working on. That will also available while you are using the D3.

This is a java script library. We need a HTML5 application that is the final result of our application. If we are adding some media query to our HTML and CSS application then it can become responsive as well. There are lots of D3 working in mobile phones (it will work differently in desktop).

Learning JavaScript on D3 is not that much easy compared to other JavaScript libraries. For that reason we have also taken this topic on D3 and it will launch soon on Udemy.

## 6.1. Final project

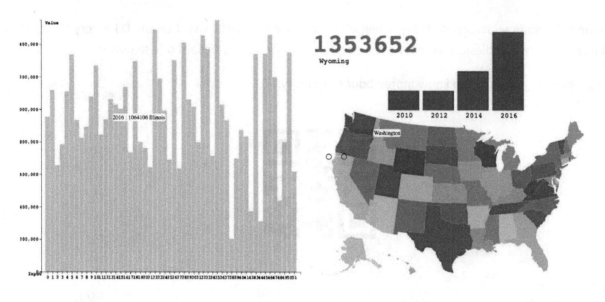

This is the final result of our application. You can also access to this link

https://preview.c9users.io/ajaytech/dataviz/D3/headStart/demo15_dashBoard.html

http://goo.gl/VyZFkX

If we open it in a browser it will show in a zoom fashion because we have designed it for bigger screens. You can use 'Ctrl' and ' – ' key to zoom out and you are able to see it clearly.

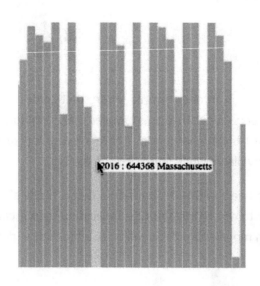

In this chart we can see that we have a population number and state in Y axis. If you drag the mouse over the bar you can see the Year, Population and the State name. This is the interaction happening once we place our mouse over any data elements.

Total Population

The value 50769516 shows the total population of United States on 2016 (Current Year). This is an estimated figure as we already told it is a model data.

In the map, the data is available if you place the mouse over each individual state. Once you click the particular state then the KPI values are changed and another bar chart appears with population growth in even number of years. This is because we have the requirement specifically for even number of years. Now when you click other state then the bar chart and KPI Values update itself. It is nice to have animation in our project so that user can see the values are changing. This is a feature that is more about interaction and representation phase. You can also add some legends to represent the different colours that mentioned in the map for additional User Experience.

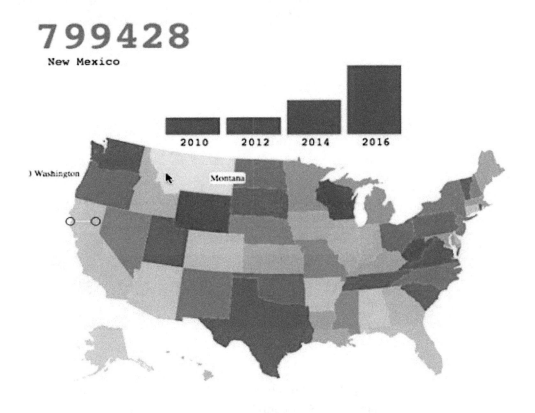

Sometimes, if we are using libraries like SAP UI5, then it has nice inbuilt charting capabilities. It adds the legends along with the data that we are adding in the Maps and Bar charts. Make sure to check out our SAP UI5 professional development in udemy.com. It is one of the most popular JavaScript libraries for enterprise application development.

Let's come back to our programming. You have access to this in cloud9 editor.

https://ide.c9.io/ajaytech/dataviz

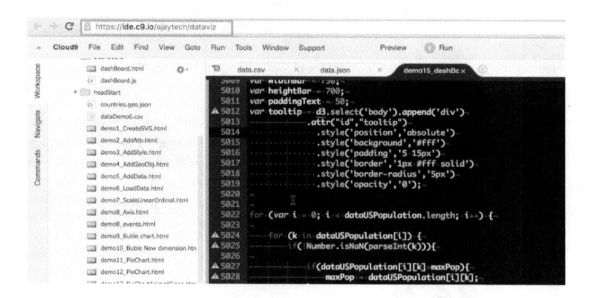

You can run this program using the run or live preview option in top of the screen. Then you are able to see the output.

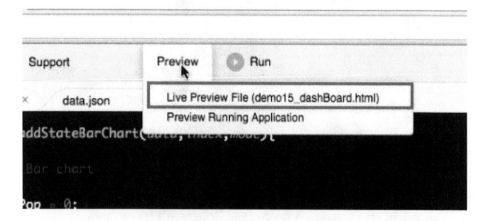

You can also see in the console by right click on the browser and select inspect element option. Inside source tab you can see the program demo15. It contains about 5000 lines of programming because of the data. The JSON data has been put in a separate file and then read in our program. However, sometime while we try in a local server there might be some security reason that our browser does not allow these data to be read by a local program. So you can copy the entire code and use it for reference purposes.

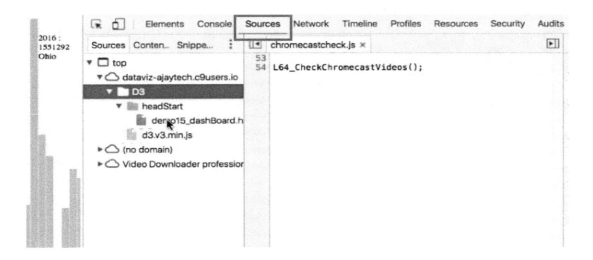

## 6.2. Code Structure

In this section we are going to see about the approach we did in current visualization design using D3. First thing we did is we understood the data. Here we have the population data we get from US census website. Also, we need to represent a map. To represent a map we need GeoJSON data. These are geographical locations. Using these we can able to draw maps.

After identifying the data we need to identify the chart that we use here. We are using bar charts. One is for showing population in all the states for current year and second one is an interactive bar chart that will show the population for current state over years. These years are even years from 2010 to 2016.

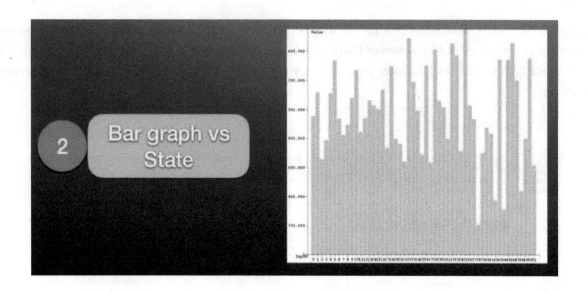

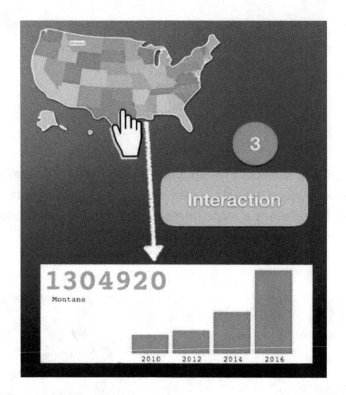

We also have a KPI field that shows the population for the current year user has selected. These are all the steps in sequence which we see here. Let's go to the D3 program and see how we are mapping these steps.

Now we are going to see the code walkthrough for the D3 program. You can skip this part if you are not a technical person or don't want to involve in technical development.

48

The codes are available in the cloud9 editor and you have access to it. To access the files in cloud, Login with your cloud9 account and open this link https://ide.c9.io/ajaytech/dataviz . There is a file name called final assignment. Simply click to open it.

```
.KPIMain{
    transform: translate(813px,-82px);
    font-size: 72px;
    fill: gray !important;
    font-weight: bold;

}
.KPIDesc{
    transform: translate(839px,-41px);
    font-size: 20px;
    color: red !important;
}
.stateChart{
    transform: translate(150px,125px);
    font-size: 20px;
    color: red !important;
}
```

## Styles for our graph

<script type="text/javascript" src="../D3/d3.v3.min.js"></script>   //Incorporating D3 library to the Application

The styles marked in the picture as number 1 are used to do styling in our graph. The placement adjustments are done using this CSS. Here we are having styles for KPI Tiles, KPI desc and Bar chart.

Next part is data. Here we are using the Geo JSON Data. In cloud9 editor you can find the

var dataGeoJSON

that contains 4000+ lines of code inside it. If you expand it the 4000+ lines of data will be shown. We can also see data in the source tab of Inspect element console window.

49

```
 29        .map{
 30            transform: translate(400px,77px);
 31        }
 32        </style>
 33    </head>
 34    <body>
 35        <script type="text/javascript">
 36    var dataGeoJSON = {[___]};
4465
4466
4467  var dataUSPopulation = [___];
4780
4781  /*
4782
4783  Code for Map
4784
4785  */
4786        //Width and height
4787        var w = 1600;
4788        var h = 800;
4789        var margin = {
4790            left:32,
4791            right:30,
4792            bottom:30,
4793            top:30
4794        }
4795        var numOfState = 52;
4796        var tooltip = d3.select('body').append('div')
```

Contains 4000+ lines of data

We are defining a polygon with some coordinates. Each state is represented as polygon with some co ordinate values. When we join the coordinates we will get the particular state in the map.

```
Elements  Console  Sources  Network  Timeline  Profiles  »

Sources  Content scr...  Snippets  ⋮   ◀  D3FinalProject....ps://ide.c9.io ×  »

▼ □ top                                    29        </style>
  ▼ ☁ preview.c9users.io                   30        </head>
    ▶ 📁 ajaytech/dataviz                   31        <body data-cloud9-id='3'>
  ▶ ☁ (no domain)                          32            <script data-cloud9-id='9' type='
  ▶ ☁ Video Downloader professional        33
                                           34            var data = {
                                           35    "type": "FeatureCollection",
                                           36    "features": [
                                           37        {
                                           38          "type": "Feature",
                                           39          "id": "01",
                                           40          "properties": {
                                           41            "name": "Alabama"
                                           42          },
                                           43          "geometry": {
                                           44            "type": "Polygon",
                                           45            "coordinates": [
                                           46              [
                                           47                [
                                           48                  -87.359296,
                                           49                  35.00118
                                           50                ],
                                           51                [
                                           52                  -85.606675,
```

After seeing the data for map then we move on to the data of US Population. It contains only 300 lines of code. It contains name of the state and the population in years as 2010, 2012, 2014, 2016. The year 2016 (Current Year) is calculated using a mathematical model.

```
var dataUSPopulation = [{
  "Name": "Alabama",
  "2010": 171889,
  "2012": 305360,
  "2014": 477249,
  "2016": 954498
},{
  "Name": "Alaska",
  "2010": 366915,
  "2012": 192876,
  "2014": 559791,
  "2016": 1119582
},{
  "Name": "Arizona",
  "2010": 161698,
  "2012": 167019,
  "2014": 328717,
  "2016": 657434
```

After this we start the coding from the map.

**Colour of the map**

```
15455
15456    var color = d3.scale.linear().domain([0,numOfState])
15457        .range(["orange","green"]);
15458
```

The syntax we shown in the picture is the scale for the map. It contains the scale from orange to green. This colour is to show the population density of the states. The orange coloured states are having less population and green coloured states having higher population. You can see the values in the bar chart provided for each state population.

**Projection**

```
15459    var projection = d3.geo.albersUsa()
15460                        .translate([w/2,h/2])
15461                        .scale([scaleOfMap]);
15462
15463    var path = d3.geo.path().projection(projection);
15464
```

The projections are D3 specific projections while using the Geo Maps.

## Creating canvas

```
15465              var svg = d3.select("body")
15466                          .append("svg")
15467                          .attr("width",w)
15468                          .attr("height",h);
```

Whenever we are using D3 we have to create a SVG Canvas.  The bar chart here drawn with this SVG Canvas.  This is the process that we need to add every element in D3. We are providing width and height as well. The margin provided here is to properly show it in devices that our users are seeing this. Basically this application is made for bigger screens and it has touch capabilities. User can touch the particular state to see the population in the chart and data value. This provides a very nice user experience.

## Fill the bar chart with colours and animation

The below code fills the bar chart with orange colour and also add some animation effects when we move the mouse over the bar chart. This comes under the interaction part. Inside the click event we calling addStateBarChart(d,i,"update"); function. This will update the state bar chart with the values of the state that is clicked. Also, after we used mouse over event and then if we get out from the state we need to use the mouseout function to remove the tooltip and change the colour back to it default state.

```
svg.selectAll("path")
    .data(data.features)
    .enter()
    .append("path")
    .attr("d",path)
    .attr("class","map")
    .style("fill",function(d,i){
        return color(i);
    }).on("mouseover",function(d){

        tooltip.transition().style("opacity",1);
        tooltip.html(d.properties.name)
        .style('left',(d3.event.pageX)+"px")
        .style('top',(d3.event.pageY)+"px");

        d3.select(this).style('opacity',0.5);

    }).on("mouseout",function(){

        d3.select(this).style('opacity',1);

    }).on("click", function(d,i){

        if(document.getElementById("stateBar").childNodes.length>0)
        {
            addStateBarChart(d,i,"update");
        }else{

            addStateBarChart(d,i,"new");
        }

    });
```

The final map with state bar chart will look like this:

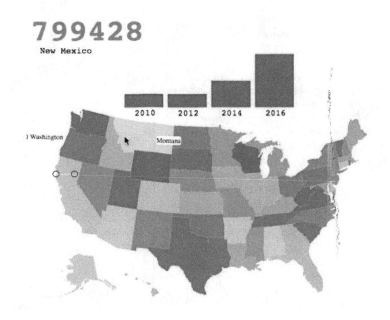

## Current year population bar chart

The current year population bar chart is the main bar chart containing the population of the current year of all the states. We are rendering the bar chart using barFirstTimeRender(); function. Inside the function we defined the tooltip that going to be used in the bar chart. The basic setting of the bar chart is defined here in parameters like Height, Width and Padding.

```
function barFirstTimeRender(){

    var maxPop = 0;
    var widthBar = 750;
    var heightBar = 700;
    var paddingText = 70;
  var tooltip = d3.select('body').append('div')
          .style('position','absolute')
          .style('background','#fff')
          .style('padding','5 15px')
          .style('border','1px #fff solid')
          .style('border-radius','5px')
          .style('opacity','0');


    for(var i=0;i<dataUSPopulation.length;i++){
        for(k in dataUSPopulation[i]){
            if(!Number.isNaN(parseInt(k))){

                if(dataUSPopulation[i][k]>maxPop){
                    maxPop = dataUSPopulation[i][k];
                }
            }
        }
    }
}
```

After defining the bar chart we need to define the scales. This is because we need to utilize the bar chart completely by giving the peak maximum value to be within the scale. After defining scale we need to add group using SVG. Using that, we draw the X and Y axes. After the axes are drawn we need to add data of US Population to plot the graph.

```
svg.append("g")
    .attr("id","xAxis")
    .call(xAxis)
    .style("stroke","#000")
    .attr("transform","translate("+paddingText+","+(heightBar)+")");

var plot = svg.append("g")
            .attr("id","barPlot")
            .selectAll()
            .data(dataUSPopulation)
            .enter()
            .append("rect")
            .attr("width",widthOfBar)
            .attr("height",function(d,i){

                return h(d["2016"]);
            })
            .style("fill","orange")
            .attr("y",function(d,i){
                return heightBar- h(d["2016"]);
            })
            .attr("x",function(d,i){
                return x(i);
            }).on('mouseover',function(d){

            tooltip.transition()
                .style('opacity',1);
                tooltip.html("2016 : "+d["2016"]+" "+d["Name"])
                    .style('left',(d3.event.pageX)+"px")
                    .style('top',(d3.event.pageY)+"px");

                d3.select(this).style('opacity',0.5);

            })
            .on('mouseout',function(){

                d3.select(this).style('opacity',1);
```

For the small population chart and KPI tile we draw the graph if it is new without any previous value and Update if it is already holding some value. The only difference for both is the enter(); keyword for new and not in update. You can see this in the function addStateBarChart(data,index,mode){}

This code shown below is for animation and transition effects.

svg.selectAll("#kpi")

.text(sBData["2016"])

.transition()

.duration(1000);


svg.selectAll("#kpiDec")

.text(sBState)

```
.transition()

.duration(1000);
```

This is the final project for data visualization. Here we saw how to create maps, bar graph, small bar graph and KPI tiles.

## 6.3. Conclusion

This was the entire data visualization course where we tried to keep all learning practical oriented. After finishing this course we have a better understanding about how a visualisation project actually runs. The different steps and actions are defined in this course. We also came to know about the purpose statements and importance of it. At the end, we use D3 to bring our design into real life.

You can also check our Learn Data Visualization and Become Data Analyst video course for accelerated learning here or use the below QR code for 50-90% off.

**Learn Data Visualization and Become Data Analyst**
UIS Community Network · SAP Experts - SAP Services, SAP Consulting, SAP Education

Learn art and science of data visualization in 7 simple steps with real world examples.

★ ★ ★ ★ ★ 4.5
(16 ratings)

● 20 lectures   ⏱ 2 hours   ┃┃┃ All Levels

# 7. Reference and bibliography

- http://alignedleft.com/work/d3-book : Interactive Data Visualization for the Web by Scott Murray
- https://d3js.org/: D3 JavaScript Libraries official documentation and API reference.
- http://www.census.gov/ : US Census government website for public data to show use case.

www.ingramcontent.com/pod-product-compliance
Lightning Source LLC
Chambersburg PA
CBHW061923080326
R17960100002B/R179601PG40689CBX00004B/1